ISBN 978-1-332-20880-7
PIBN 10298507

For support please visit www.forgottenbooks.com

1 MONTH OF
FREE
READING

at

www.ForgottenBooks.com

By purchasing this book you are eligible for one month membership to ForgottenBooks.com, giving you unlimited access to our entire collection of over 700,000 titles via our web site and mobile apps.

To claim your free month visit:

www.forgottenbooks.com/free298507

Similar Books Are Available from
www.forgottenbooks.com

Grateful acknowledgment is made for permisson to reprint such of these verses as have appeared at various times in *The Messenger* *The Pilgrim* , *The Catholic World*, *McClure's Magazine*, *The Evening Sun*, New York, *The Public Ledger*, Philadelphia, *The Eye Witness*, London, *Studies*, Dublin.

CONTENTS

THE PRIEST'S MOTHER

Flanked by serried hosts of angels multitudinous,
   Who is this that comes like an army in array?
Why does the sword of Michael gleam so glori-
   ous?
     Wherefore does Uriel with palms bestrew the
     way?

Is it one who drank of the wine-cup virginal,
   And the warmth of earth-love gladly did
     forego?
Martyr mystic-signed is this, patriarch or car-
   dinal,
     That the orbèd cherubim so tremulously glow?

Have the cohorts militant lost a blade invincible?
   Has some sinning woman from nigh the doors
     of hell,
Fighting inch by inch of the dark road terrible,
   Set her bleeding feet at last amid the asphodel?

Sister, she that shines amid the chrysoprase and
    sardius,
  Whose tears will not be stayed before the
    splendor of the East,
Is but a timid woman, frail, with worn hands
    tremulous,
  The Winner of the Smile of God, the mother of
    His priest.

He that of her very flesh was long months
    fashioning
  Now makes the Flesh of God upon the altar-
    stone;
Shall He that's fain to dwell with men be nig-
    gard of a welcoming
  To her that made the way whereby He comes
    unto His own?

THE MIST OF DREAMS

The mist of dreams is in his eyes,
　　His feet by hidden pathways go;
He is not fretted by our sighs,
　　He cannot weep for all our woe.

What should he know of human things
　　To whom the fairies gave his smiles?
Or care for human sorrowings,
　　Who travels from the Blessed Isles?

For if he knoweth of unrest,
　　'Tis that his heart is fain to be
Where those bright Islands of the Blest
　　Spread wide their fronded greenery.

And when he seemeth not to hear
　　The harshness that is human speech,
It is because unto his ear
　　Naught save that melody can reach;

That melody which is the sum
    Of rustling wings and wingéd feet,
Of lapping waves, and the drowsy hum
    Of homing bees, and laughter sweet.

And when he sees not what men do,
    Each to the other's sore despite,
It is because some fairy crew
    Flutters betwixt them and the sight.

VESPERAL

To lovelier evening wears the lovely day,
    And all the world is wrapt in cloistral hush.
    Loud from his leafy cell, the hermit thrush
Intones his *Jube, benedicere;*

A blessing on ripe meadows and full wains,
    And on the plenteous harvest of the bee,
    A blessing on still wood and fragrant lea,
Fruit of the sun, fruit of the summer rains.

Now comes sweet ease unto all weary things,
    Cattle to byre, dew unto thirsty sod;
    Fair thro' the dusk glimmer the lamps of God;
Peace and the night descend on silent wings.

THE BLESSING OF THE HARP

"O Patrick, Patrick of the Bells,
　　List to the harper of the Sidhe."
"Would you be weaving fairy spells
　　About my priestly company?"

" 'Twas I came fasting to your board,
　　You gave me food and shelter warm,
O darling of a tender Lord,
　　Is it myself would do you harm?

" 'Tis long has been your journey now,
　　Among the hills of Innisfail,
You that are sealed upon the brow
　　To be the bright torch of the Gael.

"Let you sit down in this green place
　　With your shorn sons about your knee,
And I will touch my harp a space,
　　And play the music of the Sidhe."

And first he played the hosting tune,
  Whereat the Riders of the Hills
Go forth beneath the Samhain moon
  To fetter mortals to their wills;

And next the herding tune he played,
  And all the creatures of the wood,
Both bird and beast, all unafraid,
  About the priests of Patrick stood.

And then he played the song of sleep,
  And slumber fell upon their eyes
That had such vigils long to keep:
  They slept and dreamt of Paradise.

He held them in their pleasant rest
  Until the evening shadows fell.
From every hill to east and west
  There sounded forth the vesper bell.

And then it was they stirred and woke,
  And all their weariness was fled.
Then Patrick to the harper spoke:
  "Ask what thou wilt, dear son," he
    said.

"O Patrick of the mighty heart,
    I to be saved eternally,
And thy sweet blessing on my art,
    These are the gifts I ask," said he.

"So let it be," said Patrick then,
    'Thy soul to be with Mary's Son,
And upon Erin's playing men
    The gracious blessing thou hast won:

"They to sound all the depths of tears;
    To climb the heights where angels are,
To reach the heart of him who hears
    And set it glowing like a star."

THE DARK LADY

Who were you, lady, whose black magic stayed
  The sunward soaring eagle in his flight,
And lured him to your silken leash, and made
  The sun but darkness seem beside the light
    Lurking in your dark hair and dusky eyes?
We that have wept above Verona's fair,
    And had our laughter 'neath Messina's skies
With Leonato's daughter debonair,
  We know not how nor by what English name
Men spoke of you of old in London town,
  Nor what your lover whispered, whose proud
      shame
Your faithlessness with fealty did crown,
    But, captive in his glory evermore,
    Sunward and swift, we see you mount and
      soar.

QUIS SICUT DEUS!

From term to term He reacheth mightily.
  Time to His endlessness hath set no bound;
  Its years His instants do not compass round,
Nor space containeth His immensity.
The stretched out heavens for His canopy
  He hath set up, and while the ebbing wave
  Recedeth from the boundary He gave,
He vieweth His fair world complacently.
The fiery meteor in its trackless flight
  Is orbited, and the most ancient star
That resteth on the steadfast hills at night
  Knoweth mutation, with all things that are.
    He in serene unchangefulness doth stay,
    Who no to-morrow hath nor yesterday.

THE EXILE

Hark to the sob o' the wild sea's keenin'
   Betwixt the two hearts of us, Molly aroon,
Nigh to your soul 'tis my soul is leanin'
   Over the miles that lies wide betune.

Little they think that hear me singin'
   'Tis the pain o' my heart I'm tryin' to hide,
Me that can hear the laugh o' you ringin'
   Sweet as the thrush in the green hedgeside;

Me that can see your gray eyes smilin'
   Under the shine of your hair like sloe,
Molly, 'tis you was the witch beguilin'
   To ease the hurt o' my bitter woe.

Light was the step ye had in the dancin',
   Faith, 'twas the fairies got into your feet!
When you tossed your head, love, your gray eyes
        glaucin',
   Wirra, 'tis ruined I was complete.

Gray was my heart till it went to your keepin'
   Again the beat of your own, asthore,
Joy of my sorrow, I've learned ye weepin',
   You that had never a tear of yore.

"Go," says you, "where 'tis gold is rainin',
   Many's the pocket yourself can fill,
And here will I stop without plaint or plainin'
   In the cabin you've builded again the hill."

But sorra the glint o' the gold I'm spyin',
   It's battlin' I am for sup an' bite,
For a sight o' the child in your arms I'm sighin',
   An' the sound o' my Molly's voice this night.

I can hear the droon o' the cradle swingin',
   Where ye sit in the light o' the burnin' peat.
Troth, it's the sad little song you're singin'
   An' the lilt o' the dance has left your feet.

There's threads o' white in the head you're
         bendin',
   An' wan is the hand that ye gave to me—
Sure, you're wearyin' sore for this exile's endin'
   An' the day I'll be goin' back over the sea.

THE LOST MOTHER

among the rocks one of the sea women
combing her long hair, and if he can creep up to her
unbeknownst, and steal away from her her 'cuhuleen
driuth,' which is a kind of small cap the merrows do
be wearing, she can never go back under the sea any
more at all, but must follow his bidding while ever he
has it in his keeping.

O scarlet hunter, riding past,
O hunter, do not ride so fast,
But tell me, where's my mother?—

"Nay, child, why dost thou ask of me?
Safe at the hearth should mothers be,
And thine like any other."

—While I was playing on the floor
Deep in a hollow near the door
I found a shining cap laid by.
My mother gave a piercing cry,
And snatched it up and fled away.
Though I have sought her all the day
I cannot find my mother.

O woman with the milking stool,
Standing among the grasses cool,
Hast thou not seen my mother?

"What like is thy mother, lad?"
—A stripëd petticoat she had,
Her snooded hair is soft as silk,
She's whiter in the face than milk,
My lost, sweet mother.

"I saw a poor mad thing go down
By yonder highway to the town,
I saw none other.
But oh, her hair was streaming wild,
Sure, frenzy was upon her, child,
    And she was not thy mother."

O friar, in thy long rough gown,
Say in what corner of the town
I'll find my mother.

"What is thy mother's name, poor
        boy?"
My father always called her Joy.

14

"It hath the ring of Heathenesse,
But to all creatures in distress
Lord Christ is Brother.
In the churchyard an hour ago
I saw a witch-girl crouching low.
But oh, she fell to weeping sore
For that she feared the cross I wore.
I'll dry thy tears and lead thee home.
Good mothers have no wish to roam."
　—Nay, I must find my mother.

　O fisher, coming in from sea,
Lay by the oar and answer me.
O hast thou seen my mother?

　"Nay, but I saw, upon my life,
'Mong yonder rocks a merrow wife,
With long locks streaming in the sun.
She saw the billows shoreward run,
She heard the splashing of my oar.
Wildly she glanced along the shore.
She flung her foam-white arms on high.
She cried a weird and wailing cry,
And leaped and vanished in the sea.
I crossed the brow and breast of me,
And thanked the Maker of my life
That I've a christened maid to wife.

WHEN YOU ARE OLD

"Quand vous serez bien vieille."—RONSARD.

When you are very old, with snowy hair,
  Sitting beside the fire at candle-light,
  You will remember all my rhymes aright,
And murmur, "Ronsard sang when I was fair."
  Then at your side no drowsy little maid,
Leaning adream above her tambour-frame,
But will arouse at mention of my name,
    Knowing your name with deathless praise
      arrayed.
I shall lie under earth, my restless ghost,
Beneath the myrtle shade shall wander lost,
  You will crouch cold the dying flame beside.
  Ah, then, be kind to-day; no longer wait
  To weep for my spent love and your harsh
      pride,
    Gather life's roses ere it be too late.

THE BIRDS OF AENGUS OG

In my young youth 'twas I that heard them
         calling,
The birds of Aengus, Aengus Ever-Young,
While the pale light between the hills was falling,
I heard the hounds of elfland giving tongue.

Then of my lot no comfort was I getting,
Low seemed your eaves to me and strait your
         door;
After the birds of Aengus was I fretting,
And fain was I to hear their call once more.

Though by rough ways my eager feet went
         straying
Far and away from all the haunts of men,
Near fairy rings and lonely raths delaying,
Never I won to sight of them again.

At long and last I see their blue wings gleaming,
Soft comes the call that woo'd me to my quest;
Under your eaves the bright birds of my dream-
  ing,
The birds of Aengus Og, have built their nest.

THE FIDDLER

I know 'tis low the August moon is ridin',
In lacy clouds her face she's hidin',
　　An' smilin', too, the clouds between,
For in the balmy Summer weather,
The colleens and the lads together
　　Are dancin' on the village green.

I hear them near an' whirlin' gaily by me,
Many's the love-word whispered nigh me,
　　It's then we smile, the moon an' I;
Sure, lave them alone to their romancin',
It's young they are, an' why not dancin'?
　　The old have time enough to sigh.

What sigh had I when youth was golden?
Faith, an' to none was I beholden,
　　Nor thought to pay the fiddler's fee,
Now I'm dark an' the youth-time ended,
Alone an' feeble an' unfriended,
　　Who is the fiddler?　Who but me?

THE FLOWER VENDOR

Now is the winter gone! Here's one that dares
Flaunt in the face of gusty March his wares.
Though she with hoyden turmoil fill the street,
Jacinths are here, and here's arbutus sweet,
Still wet, and fragrant of the underwood.
Up then, poor heart! Let you have hardihood.
Somewhere this poet in the dusty coat
Has seen earth laugh, has heard the throstle's
        note.
What matter winds? Let them go railing on.
Spring's here, Spring's here! The winter's gone!

OMNISCIENCE

Thou seest the under side of every leaf,
  The arteries of earth are bare to Thee,
  Before Thee hell is naked, every sea
Is crystal, every garnered sheaf,
Grain upon grain, Thou knowest; not a blade
  Of withered grass the wind blows vagrantly
  But at Thy nod; the nest-woof Thou dost see,
The speckling of the egg within it laid.

The wheeling planets Thou dost call by name,
  There is no star so lost in utter space
  Thou markest not its shining and its place,
And every hearth and every altar flame.
And souls of men are as a page outspread
  Whereon Thou readest both of good and
      base:—
  What falling rock shall hide us from Thy face?
May we escape Thy glance, though we be dead?

Yea, but Thou seest that our frame is weak,
  And that the thing we do is that we hate,
  Thou seest that we weep when it is late,
And wound the heart that loves us when we
    speak,
Thou knowest that our portion is but tears,
  We love to lose, are little and not great;—
  With Thy large glance Thou readest all our
    state,
And wilt be patient of our empty years.

THE LESSER PEACE

Before my glass is wholly run
I ask a span of quiet years,
When I may wind the thread I've spun,
Learn laughter and remember tears.

A season of good fellowship
Beneath the sky with wind and rain,
When buckling on my shallow scrip
I leave behind the ways of pain.

I ask a little garden close
Wherein to learn the common grace
Of herb and flow'r, before the snows
Make pale the warm earth's comely face;

A lesser peace before the great,
A little while to court the sun,
To sit with folded hands and wait
The coming of the Silent One.

SILENCE IN HEAVEN

The citherns lie with muted strings,
  And hushed is Heaven's psaltery,
No seraph stirs his flaming wings,
  No wave disturbs the crystal sea.

Six spirits stand before God's face,
  Where seven are wont to minister,
For Gabriel has left his place,
  And sped him as God's messenger.

The praising multitudes are dumb.
  All Heaven waits with trancëd breath,
Until the answering word shall come
  From Mary's house in Nazareth.

THE FORESEEING OF DEIRDRE

Deirdre of the Yellow Hair,
  What's on you that you sigh?
All flowery are the apple-trees,
The blossoms rain about your knees,
  The lark is in the sky;
Deirdre of the Yellow Hair,
You that have silken gowns to wear,
And gold and gems beyond compare,
  What's on you that you sigh?

My grief! to see the lark's far flight
  Beyond the orchard wall,
And I that cannot leave your sight,
  Nor stray beyond your call.
It's far my feet shall travel yet,
And spray of many seas shall wet
  My shining yellow hair,
But narrow shall my housing be,
Down where the waves of Ireland's sea
  The sands of Ulster wear.

Deirdre of the Slender Hands,
　What's on you that you weep?
All tangled lies your scarlet skein,
While your slow tears, like summer rain,
　Betwixt your fingers creep;
Deirdre of the Slender Hands,
Make haste and wind your scattered strands,
Make haste and sew your broidered bands.
　What's on you that you weep?

My grief! to see the crimson thread
*　Like blood upon the ground.*
It's I am heavy with the dread.
*　Of the long skein unwound.*
I'll have my fill of laughter yet,
Red wine my redder lips shall wet,
*　And I'll be mad with mirth,*
But oh, the bitter tears I'll shed
When I shall crouch among the dead
*　Upon the blood-wet earth.*

Deirdre of the Dreaming Eye,
　What's on you that you smile?
The bitter tempest howls without,
And blows the naked boughs about,
　And you to laugh the while.
Deirdre of the Dreaming Eye,
While all the flowers of summer die,
And round the dun the bleak winds sigh,
　What's on you that you smile?

Oh, saw you not the spent stag's blood
   Run crimson on the snow?
And saw you not the raven's brood
   That drank the ruddy flow?
I'll walk the hills of sorrow yet,
And sorrow's rain my cheek shall wet,
     And sorrow's wind blow chill,
But I will mind my love's dark head,
His brow so white, his cheek so red,
     And smile at sorrow still.

"THE BIRDS OF THE AIR HAVE NESTS

O, high builds the swallow,
And low builds the wren,
But where is the house of the
Son of God
Among the sons of men?

There's the rock for the sea-gull
For the linnet the sod,
But where is the throne of the
Lord of Hosts?
Even our hearts, O God.

THE PIPES OF MANANAAN

Weird is the golden glamour falling
  Across the misty slopes of dawn,
And elfin pipes are faintly calling,
  The magic pipes of Mananaan.

Come forth, O King of Ireland's daughter,
  Come out into the dusk of morn,
Come, for the King of the Under Water
  Is waiting beside the twisted thorn.

The way his three fair cows went lowing
  The length of many a weary mile,
Broad and brown are the three roads going
  From end to end of Erin's isle.

In his cap is a sea-gull's feather,
  He made the roads for his wandering,
For you and him and song together
  To be abroad in the pleasant Spring.

Who would a crown of gold be wearing
   When he is clad in beggar's gear?
Who for the wealth of the world be caring
   When Mananaan is piping near?

MARIANSON

(From the French)

"Marianson, my lady fair,
Lend me your three gold rings to wear."

Marianson, all undistrest,
Has lent her rings at his behest.

Then has he ta'en the trinkets three
Unto the goldsmith hastily.

"O craftie smith, I pray you make
Three golden rings for Mary's sake.

"Let them be fairly wrought upon
Like these three rings of Marianson."

When he has held the rings of gold
He mounts him on his charger bold.

The first he meets upon the way
It is the lady's lord so gay.

"Now God thee keep, thou hardy knight!
What gladness makes thine eyes so bright?

"It is because the love I've won
Of that high lady, Marianson."

"Thou liest, knave, and this I swear
By my love's rings that she doth wear."

"Ah, well, believe but as thou list!
Behold the rings her lips have kist!"

When he the carven gold has seen
Stark is he fallen on the green.

There for three nights and days he's lain,
Nor meat nor drink to ease his pain.

Then up he's risen suddenly,
And to his good steed given knee.

His mother, from the turret high,
Marks where he rides, and loud doth cry·

"My lady daughter, knowest thou
It is thy husband cometh now?

"Yet rides he not here lovingly;
As one anangered sore rides he.

"But take thy young son on thine arm,
The babe his father's sight will charm.

"Good morrow, son, receive thine heir,
And say what name thou'lt have him bear."

He's snatched the young child from her breast
And dashed it 'gainst the oaken chest.

And then he's ta'en his wife so pale
And dragged her at his horse's tail.

There's not a tree in all the wood
Unwetted by the lady's blood.

"Now may'st thou rot upon the mould,
But say where are thy rings of gold?"

"Take thou the key bound at my wrist,
And find the rings thy lips have kist."

O when the golden rings he sees,
Low does he fall upon his knees:

"Is there none skilled in surgery
May make thy body whole for me?"

"None is so skilled in surgery
To make my body whole for thee.

"My need is now a slender thing,
But thread and needles let them bring.

"And let a white shroud fashioned be
Wherein to wrap and bury me."

BROTHER JUNIPER

As unto Francis Poverty,
So Folly was a bride to thee.
Not the jade that fashions quips
For the smiles of mocking lips,
And in the face of stony Death
Capers till she's out of breath,
But the maid that moves and sings
About divinely foolish things,
She that gives her substance all
For love, and laughs to find it small,
She that drew God's Son to be
A butt, a jest on Calvary,
And 'neath the leper's guise doth know
The King in his incognito.

The world is grown too wise, and we
Go our sad ways sensibly.
O, would that our lean souls might win
Some grace of thine, God's harlequin,

Whose days were lavished like fool's gold
Upon His pleasures manifold.
"Would God," cried Francis, on his knees,
"I had a forest of such trees!"

A BALLADE OF LOST ISLANDS

"There are no more Blessed Islands."—NIETZSCHE.

Ye sail the charted seas in vain
    And seek in vain for that dim strand
No man of you shall see again,
    The isles where Morgain held command,
Where Blessed Brendan lowered sail
    And lingered near the pleasant shore;
Give over, for the search must fail,
    The Blessed Islands are no more.

They that in Maildún's curragh went
    Far off beheld the happy throng,
In radiant dress, with gems besprent,
    And lent their voices to the song;
Now no man hears that fairy tune
    Ring out above the billow's roar
No eye beholds them 'neath the moon,
    The Blessed Islands are no more.

How many ships have faced the morn,
    And put 'mid shoutings out to sea,
To come again with canvas torn
    And tales of outland wizardry!
And some have come with piled gold,
    And some with strange beasts many score,
But none returns with empty hold,
    The Blessed Islands are no more.

ENVOY

Mates, get ye home in wealth and pride;
    No mystery from shore to shore
Eludes you on the waters wide,
    The Blessed Islands are no more.

THE DESERTERS

Long and long and long ago,
  In the sunny weather,
Youth and Love and Song and I
  Took the road together.

Youth was all for dancing then,
  Love was all for laughter,
Song and I on dancing feet,
  Laughing, followed after.

Ho, for the rest beneath the hedge,
  'Mid the wayside flowers,
Ho, for the dust upon the coat
  Ho, for summer showers.

But there came a night when Youth
  Fled while I was sleeping;
Then must Love steal after him
  Though he left me weeping.

Still the hedgerows shelter me,
  Ragged coat I'm wearing,
But sweet Song my fellow is,
  Wheresoe'er I'm faring.

THE HARP OF THREE STRINGS

The King of the world no more, no more
  Shall swing his dauntless blade,
The foe to hear his battle roar
  No more shall flee afraid.

There came unto the level strand
  A woman of the West;
He gave her the ring from off his hand,
  The heart from out his breast.

Of three strings was the harp she bore
  At her white shoulder slung.
She sat her on the sandy floor
  And elfin songs she sung.

And when she struck the iron string
  Black sorrow on him fell,
And from his eyes such tears did spring
  As weep the woes of hell.

And when the string of bronze she played
  The joy of all the earth
Was loosed upon him, and he prayed
  He might not die of mirth;

But when beneath her finger tips
  The silver string did sound
He looked no more at his tall ships
  Nor at his baying hound.

Nor fight nor hunt can reach his ear,
  Nor mortal minstrelsy,
Who smiles forevermore to hear
  The harping of the Sidhe.*

*Sidhe, pronounced *Shee*, i. e., fairies.

THE HOUSEWIFE'S PRAYER

Lady, who with tender ward
Didst keep the house of Christ the Lord,
Who didst set forth the bread and wine
Before the Living Wheat and Vine,
Reverently didst make the bed
Whereon was laid the holy Head
That such a cruel pillow prest
For our behoof, on Calvary's crest;
Be beside me while I go
About my labors to and fro.
Speed the wheel and speed the loom,
Guide the needle and the broom,
Make my bread rise sweet and light,
Make my cheese come foamy white,
Yellow may my butter be
As cowslips blowing on the lea.
Homely though my tasks and small,
Be beside me at them all.
Then when I shall stand to face
Jesu in the judgment place,
To me thy gracious help afford,
Who art the Handmaid of the Lord.

SECURITY

"I keep thee full surely."
—Rev. of JULIANA OF NORWICH.

Secure amid the engulfing floods I hold thee,
    Serene amid the storm;
Within My arms I gather and enfold thee
    Out of the path of harm.

Within the pleasance of My love I hide thee,
    The secret of My face.
No wrong may overcome, no ill betide thee
    Beyond My cloistering grace.

Out of the press of men I call and choose thee,
    I bind thee with My bands.
Then be thou not dismayed; how should I lose
      thee
    Who grave thee in My hands?

O CLAVIS DAVID[1]

O Key of David, come!
   Shut is my door and locked.
   In vain Thy grace hath knocked,
There is no room, no room.

Fear visiteth the stars,
   Suns from Thy pathway flee,
   And yet, O Israel's Key,
Fast hold my bolts and bars.

So narrow is my door,
   Its lintel is so low;
   How should a King's feet go
Across so mean a floor?

O Key of David's line,
   Thou makest Thyself small,
   The bolts and barriers fall,
And all the house is Thine.

O David's royal Key,
   Without are strife and wars;
   Make fast the bolts and bars,
And lock me in with Thee.

MILITARISM

"Peace, peace; and there was no peace."

Not at my ease in the tent nor adream in the
    hall,
  Not with my sword at my thigh and my lance
    at rest,
But full in the shock of the fray on the field let
    me fall,
  With the Conqueror's voice in my ears, and
    my eyes on His crest;

Where the horses flounder and plunge and the
    captains shout,
  And the Conqueror rides in the van on His
    stallion white;—
Whether I fall in the breach or go down in the
    rout,
  Let there be neither parley nor truce, let me
    die in the fight.

THE VISITATION

Now all the birds of Galilee
Sing roundelays in every tree,
For Mary goes to the hill country.

And all the furry creatures shy
That in the thickets dwell, draw nigh,
To see God's Mother passing by.

The lily cups like censers nod,
And spread their perfumes all abroad.
For honor to the Bride of God.

Now whence is this, Elizabeth?
At thy door-sill halt sin and death,
For Mary comes from Nazareth.

O thou whose barren age was blest,
Teach my dull heart to know its Guest,
And leap, like John, within my breast.

THE IRISH AT THE FRONT

Because of the deaths of our fathers
　　In ancient years,
Because of the blood of the children,
　　The women's tears;

Because of the blasted farmstead,
　　The broken latch,
The foot of the spy on the hearthstone,
　　The burning thatch;

Because of the bush and the gallows,
　　The felon's cell,
Because of the fine and the famine,
　　"Connaught or Hell;"

For these have we left the boreens,
　　The Irish sky,
These are the things, O England,
　　For which we die.

For these are the fields of Flanders
    With our blood wet;
O England, let you remember
    What we forget!

BESIDE THE CRIB

Thy little hands against my heart
  Are as strong bands to bind me,
So tiny and so frail Thou art,
  And come so far to find me.

How soft about Thy baby brow
  The tendrilled hair is twining!
Close may I lean above Thee now,
  Since Thou hast hid Thy shining.

My eyes run down with tears to see
  Thy upturned face beguiling,
And rapture in the soul of me
  Is fed upon Thy smiling.

If Thou wert not so little, Lord,
  How should I come so near Thee?
For thinking on Thy thundered word
  I could not choose but fear Thee.

Thy saints have cried aloud to Thee
  In terror of Thy smiting,
Lest Thy sharp spear of equity
  Thou seize for sin's requiting.

But when I see Thy nestling feet,
  Thy dimpled fingers moving,
My spirit laughs to find Thee sweet
  My heart is faint with loving.

O God Who art my Brotherkin,
  O Child Who art my Father,
O Lamb and Shepherd leading in
  The straylings Thou dost gather,

How may Thy slender shoulders bear
  The weight of all my sinning?
How wilt Thou take on Thee the care
  And pain of my soul's winning?

THE LITTLE BLACK ROSE

Not fled is all thine ancient glory,
    Dark Roisin dear,
Nor vanished all thy knights of story,
    Unknown to fear.

Still hast thou lovers fit for wearing
    The blade of Finn,
Still are their hearts afire with daring
    Thy weal to win.

Our days have heard their songs beguiling,
    Their dauntless words
Have seen again thy wan lips smiling
    Through flash of swords.

Once more the warriors stir in sleeping,
    Their horses fret,
To hear again, 'mid sound of weeping,
    The dread "Not yet."

Not yet the hour of thine adorning,
    O dear Dark Head,
Nor ended yet thy bitter mourning
    For heroes dead.

Yet art thou peerless past denying,
    To scorn thee's vain,
Since such as these go forth to dying
    For love, not gain.

DOMINUS TECUM

"Daughter, I was in thy heart."
           —*Revelations of St. Catherine of Siena.*

Where were You, Lord, when 'mid my sore
      alarms,
Benighted in bleak ways, I groped and cried,
Before I found the shelter of Your arms?
    —I journeyed at your side.

Where were You, Lord, when Sorrow climbed
      my stair,
And many a wan-eyed vigil with me kept,
When I could find no solace anywhere?
    —I watched with you and wept.

Where were You, Lord, when Sin and I drew
      near
And smiled upon each other, set apart,
Before I turned with loathing and with fear?
    —I smiled within your heart.

CPSIA information can be obtained at www.ICGtesting.com
Printed in the USA
BVOW06s0418091015

421363BV00008B/142/P